# Talk of the Tamarinds

an anthology of poetry for
secondary schools

*edited by* A.N. Forde

Edward Arnold (Publishers) Limited, London
Columbus Publishers Limited, Trinidad

First published 1971
by Edward Arnold (Publishers) Ltd.,
41 Maddox Street,
London, W1R 0AN

ISBN: 0 7131 1672 2

Printed in Great Britain by
Richard Clay (The Chaucer Press), Ltd.,
Bungay, Suffolk

# CONTENTS

Introduction

*The lighter side of life*

*Nature, the giver, the teacher*

# INTRODUCTION

Many years ago I wrote a poem called *Sea Bird*.

I had gone to the beach for a sea bath, but it turned out to be a dull, grey day and I didn't bathe. There was no one to share my company on the wide stretch of sand.

I sat on a clump of vegetation and listened to the waves striking the rocks.

Then I saw it : a bird rising from an area of rocks and shingle, alone, circling in the air, climbing, then returning to the barren corner of the seashore.

The bird seemed happy at its freedom.

I tried to capture this feeling in a short poem I wrote about the incident. Here are some lines from that poem :

> Your nest left huddled
> In the ear of a rock
> Mid the blast and wrack
> Of fretful billows
> Clamouring to be heard
> You ride into the silence of the sky.
>
> And far below you
> As you soar
> I envy your freedom
> From the tug of time
> Your glory
> In the welfare of the air.

There were three things I was trying for in that poem : a flow of the words to simulate the flying of the bird, a harmony in the vowel sounds and generally a choice of words to convey the sentiment of happiness in the bird.

Look at the word *ear* in the second line of the extract above. I don't know if it strikes you as odd to speak of

'the ear of a rock'. I had at first used the word 'crevice'
but it seemed too impersonal a word. Like using the word
'hole', though 'crevice' was certainly better than 'hole'
to my thinking.

The word 'ear' seemed to me to carry more personal
significance than 'crevice'.

Also it had a sound- and sight-relationship with other
words in the poem : 'h*ear*d' and 'welf*are* of the *air*'.

Take the word 'wrack'. The old word 'wrack' seemed
to me better than 'wreck'. 'Rock' followed by wrack
seemed softer than 'rock' followed by 'wreck' and I
wished to tone down the harshnesses.

What of the vowels? R*i*de into the s*i*lence of the sky.
These I tried to harmonize.

Well, I have talked about this merely to show you how
much can go into a simple – even unsuccessful – poem.

Why does the poet do this?

In the words of the English poet George Macbeth 'The
poet constantly wishes to achieve control over experience
and words in such a way that you can make something
absolutely new'.

Aimé Cesaire, the poet from Martinique, one of our
Caribbean islands, expresses this urge of the poet to be a
part of new experience as follows :

'I want to re-discover the secret of great speech and of
great burning. I want to say storm. I want to say river. I
want to say tornado. I want to say leaf. I want to say tree.
I want to be soaked by every rainfall, moistened by every
dew.'

Each poem, you see, tries to bring together the special
feelings of the poet and the peculiar qualities and
ingredients of language to define the experience in a way
that it has never been defined before.

I hope you will find that the poems in this anthology,
many of them written by persons born in the Caribbean,
bring new views of life to you as you read them.

A. N. FORDE

# The sea and ships

## A SEA-CHANTEY

*Derek Walcott*

*Là, tout n'est qu'ordre et beauté,*
*Luxe, calme, et volupté.*

Anguilla, Adina,
Antigua, Cannelles,
Andreuille, all the I's,
Voyelles, of the liquid Antilles,
The names tremble like needles
Of anchored frigates,
Yachts tranquil as lilies,
In ports of calm coral,
The lithe, ebony hulls
Of strait-stitching schooners,
The needles of their masts
That thread archipelagoes
Refracted embroidery
In feverish waters
Of the sea-farer's islands,
Their shorn, leaning palms,
Shaft of Odysseus,
Cyclopic volcanoes,
Creak their own histories,
In the peace of green anchorage;
Flight, and Phyllis,
Returned from the Grenadines,
Names entered this sabbath,
In the post-clerk's register;
Their baptismal names,
The sea's liquid letters,

Repos donnez a cils ...
And their blazing cargoes
Of charcoal and oranges;
Quiet, the fury of their ropes.

Daybreak is breaking
On the green chrome water,
The white herons of yachts
Are at sabbath communion,
The histories of schooners
Are murmured in coral,
Their cargoes of sponges
On sandspits of islets,
Barques white as white salt
Of acrid Saint Maarten,
Hulls crusted with barnacles,
Holds foul with great turtles,
Whose ship-boys have seen
The blue heave of Leviathan,
A sea-faring, Christian,
And intrepid people.

Now an apprentice washes his cheeks
With salt water and sunlight.

In the middle of the harbour
A fish breaks the Sabbath
With a silvery leap.
The scales fall from him
In a tinkle of church-bells;
The town streets are orange
With the week-ripened sunlight,
Balanced on the bowsprit
A young sailor is playing
His grandfather's chantey
On a trembling mouth-organ.
The music curls, dwindling
Like smoke from blue galleys,
To dissolve near the mountains.

2

The music uncurls with
The soft vowels of inlets,
The christening of vessels,
The titles of portages,
The colours of sea-grapes,
The tartness of sea-almonds,
The alphabet of church-bells,
The peace of white horses,
The pastures of ports,
The litany of islands,
The rosary of archipelagoes,
Anguilla, Antigua,
Virgin of Guadeloupe,
And stone-white Grenada
Of sunlight and pigeons,
The amen of calm waters,
The amen of calm waters,
The amen of calm waters.


## THE VESSELS

*Owen Campbell*


Since morning on the bright brass of the bay
They stuck in groups, moulded in clusters there,
Tackle and cable caught taut by the masts,
All twiny and wiry entangled
Where
They might have stood for twenty or more years.

Each splash is a white, green, or blue answer
From sky or sun and the leaf-painted cape,
And stuck still, set in flashing and sparkle
Were nearly all the ships like sisters here,
And the drizzle
Of shadow falling on water between.

Sleek as birds, fine and delicate as dames
'Angela', 'Gardenia', and 'Lady Dove',
Schooner 'May Olive', sloops tidy, at ease,
Coy little yachts, shy at each boy-chuckle
Of the breeze
All at anchor, all shapely and slender.

And at evening, these tall virgins are there
Assembled for prayer in the goldlight,
Or meditation where sea is catcher
For tints, or cares softly for noteless shape
And shimmer,
Until night comes and each should bear her lamp.

*　　　*　　　*

Stir comes quickly in the quietest of places,
The dozing girl is soon awake;
So on the sea the sudden wail
Of drawn anchor, twine and tackle
Cuts the still dream; and the sly sail
Creeps slowly skywards with the song
Of sailormen, and the motion,
Soft as a sweetheart's parting, for the ocean,

For islands and calm bays all in the same round sea,
South, with the wind and hundred bags
Of traffickers' sweet fruit and yam,
Northwards, for rich salt and timber
Willing and lithe in the firm arm
Of the urgent air; or slothful
And sad in great windless spaces
On the solid sea's calm places.

The liner crosses with smoking, and in the haze
Far off is a ghost of the sea
Fleeing in the white blown sheet,
Or still as sentinel of wastes
Crowding the moment like a fleet

4

Omen, frightening, come and gone;
Or fluttering as a joy away,
White sail grained in the far mist grey.

After long knifing the spray and untired wave,
Battling the wilful drift of tides,
Passing green islets on the way,
Wheeling, finding a path again,
Tacking, churning the foam and spray,
Tracing long lines white across capes,
Ship comes home to port, sails flapping,
Glad as drum-joy after fighting.

*     *     *

So we, blustering through hours
Must leave multiple track-lines in the dark
In our close hunt for the minute respite
Before next voyages.


## FRAGMENT OF MEMORY

*Martin Carter*


We have a sea on this shore
Whole waves of foam groan out perpetually.
In the ships coming, in the black slaves dying
In the hot sun burning down –
We bear a mark no shower of tears can shift.
On the bed of the ocean bones alone remain
rolling like pebbles drowned in many years.

From the beginning of ships
there was always someone who wept when sails were lost.

Perhaps the brown Phoenician woman cried
and cried again because a ship went down ...

Or then some Grecian boy with swollen eyes
looked for his father only saw the sea ...

There must be some tale telling of a wife
who bred a son upon the Spanish coast
then died before her sailor husband came ...

From the beginning of ships
the sea was always making misery
water and wave, water and wave again.

On life the ocean stained with memory
where are the ships?
but none can say today.

The ships are gone and men remain to show
with a strong black skin what course those keels had cut.


## THE SEA

*James Reeves*


The sea is a hungry dog,
Giant and grey.
He rolls on the beach all day.
With his clashing teeth and shaggy jaws
Hour upon hour he gnaws
The rumbling, tumbling stones.
And 'Bones, bones, bones, bones!'
The giant sea dog moans,
Licking his greasy paws.

6

And when the night wind roars
And the moon rocks in the stormy cloud,
He bounds to his feet and snuffs and sniffs,
Shaking his wet sides over the cliffs,
And howls and hollos long and loud.

But in quiet days in May or June,
When even the grasses on the dune
Play no more their reedy tune.
With his head between his paws
He lies on the sandy shores,
So quiet, so quiet, he scarcely snores.


## THE SURFER

*Judith Wright*

He thrust his joy against the weight of the sea;
climbed through, slid under those long banks of foam –
(hawthorn hedges in spring, thorns in the face stinging).
How his brown strength drove through the hollow and coil
of green-through weirs of water!
Muscle of arm thrust down long muscle of water;
and swimming so, went out of sight
where mortal, masterful, frail, the gulls went wheeling
in air as he in water, with delight.

Turn home, the sun goes down; swimmer, turn home.
Last leaf of gold vanishes from the sea-curve.
Take the big roller's shoulder, speed and swerve;
Come to the long beach home like a gull diving.

For on the sand the grey-wolf lies snarling,
cold twilight wind splits the waves' hair and shows
the bones they worry in their wolf-teeth. O, wind blows

and sea crouches on sand, fawning and mouthing;
drops there and snatches again, drops and again snatches
its broken toys, its whitened pebbles and shells.


## THE BEACH

*Robert Graves*


Louder than gulls the little children scream
Whom fathers haul into the jovial foam;
But others fearlessly rush in, breast high,
Laughing the salty water from their mouths –
Heroes of the nursery.

The horny boatman, who has seen whales
And flying fishes, who has sailed as far
As Demerara and the Ivory Coast,
Will warn them, when they crowd to hear his tales,
That every ocean smells alike of tar.


## THE SHIP

*Sir John Squire*


There was no song nor shout of joy
    Nor beam of moon or sun,
When she came back from the voyage
    Long ago begun;

But twilight on the waters
  Was quiet and grey,
And she glided steady, steady and pensive,
  Over the open bay.

Her sails were brown and ragged,
  And her crew hollow-eyed,
But their silent lips spoke content
  And their shoulders pride;
Though she had no captives on her deck,
  And in her hold
There were no heaps of corn or timber
  Or silks or gold.


## THE BEACHCOMBER

*W. H. Oliver*


Tall ships were wrecked here and exotic cargoes
Spilled on the beach, not yet for the wave
And rock to disfigure, nor inquisitive gull to discard,
But for his delectation. For the space of an hour
Between tide and conquering tide
He could walk among an old world's refuse,
Decking worn smooth and bone fretted on rock,
Metal turned golden red and shaped like small roses,
Run his fingers through them until the whorled shell,
The ocean's own grace, became part of his own fancy;
And then walk homewards as the tide gathered
With his head full of ghosts.

Then the wild wave carried
Shells, bone and roses into a common fortune.

Walking homewards he knew that the time was soon
    coming
When the wave would gather him too
And his long bones mingle
With that old, imaginable world
Of roses hammered from gold and dyed with his own blood.

# Doing things, shaping life

## FOR CHRISTOPHER COLUMBUS

*A. J. Seymour*

3

And so they came upon San Salvador,
When the dawn broke, the island floated ahead
Thick with the wind-swayed trees upon the shore.

Men shouted and cried for joy to see instead
Of waving waste of ocean, that tangled green,
The shrub and tree all dark with the bright red

Of foreign flowers on the leaves' glossy sheen.
The ships cast anchor with a triple crash
That startled seabirds, whirred them winging, lean

Neck stretched, to bank upon the trees. The splash
Died quickly into winking patches of foam
Widening out upon the swelling wash.

Men crowded boats. The Indians watched them come,
Riding upon the breaking waves to shore.
Until they feared and ran to find their homes

Deep in the woods. His mail Columbus wore,
The glittering cloaked in scarlet, and he sprang
Out on the sea-stained sand and kneeling, poured

His heart to God. On that beach dawn there hangs
A heavy caul of reverence, for kneeling there
The others felt vast choirs of angels sang

Within their hearts to hallow them many a year.
Rising up sworded, Columbus spoke again
And claimed San Salvador for the royal pair
Fernando and Queen Isabel of Spain.

4

He dreamed not that the ocean would bear ships
Heavy with slaves in the holds, to spill their seed
And fertilize new islands under whips

Of many nail-knotted thongs – dreamt not indeed
Massive steel eagles would keep an anxious watch
For strange and glittering fish where now was weed.

He knew not that a world beneath his touch
Springing to life would flower in cities and towns
Over two continents, nor guessed that such

A ferment of civilisation was set down
Would overshadow Europe whence he came,
He could not dream how on the nations' tongue

Discovery would marry with his name.
That to these simple Indians his ships brought doom
For cargo; that the world was not the same

Because his vision had driven him from home
And that as architect of a new age
The solid world would build upon his poem.

5

And so the day beginning.
                              In the vast Atlantic
The sun's eye blazes over the edge of ocean
And watches the islands in a great bow curving
From Florida down to the South American coast

Behind these towers in a hollow of ocean
Quiet from the Trade Winds lies the Caribbean
With the long shadows on her breathing bosom
Thrown from the islands in the morning sun.

And as the wind comes up, millions of palm trees
Weave leaves in rhythm as the shaft of sunlight
Numbers the islands till it reaches Cuba
Leaps the last neck of water in its course.


# HOMAGE TO PLANTERS

*Frank Collymore*


'Tis said they are a grasping lot
      Who grudge the peasant all;
Who chiefly live to fill their guts,
      And upon whom the call
Of all the finer things of life
      Is never known to fall;

Who only think and talk about
      Foreign manure and rains
And all the other things that serve
      To feed their greedy canes;
Who every night squat themselves down
      To gloat upon their gains.

Perhaps they do. I do not know
      Much about sugar-kings;
But I salute with gratitude
      The loving care which wrings
Such beauty from the soil and o'er
      Our land its patchwork flings.

# ROAD TO LACOVIA

*A. L. Hendricks*

This is a long, forbidding road, a narrow,
hard aisle of asphalt under
a high gothic arch of bamboos.
Along it a woman drags a makeshift barrow
in slanting rain, and thunder:
a thin woman who wears no shoes.

This is St. Elizabeth, a hard parish
to work; but when you are born
on land, you want to work that land.
Nightfall comes here swift and harsh and deep, but garish
flames of lightning show up torn
cheap clothing barely patched, and

a face patterned by living. Every sharp line
of this etching has the mark
of struggle. To the eye, unyielding
bleak earth has brought her close to famine;
yet through this wild descent of dark
this woman dares to walk, and sing.

# VOLTA

*Edward Brathwaite*

My lord, all this time since we left
Walata, you have led these people. Are you not
tired?

14

I am very tired, Munia. My head
aches, my feet
are weary; sometimes
the light seems to sing before my face.
My blood cries out for rest.

But still you won't rest
you won't give up. Can't we
stop here? Have we
not travelled enough?

The young men murmur, El
Hassan; the women
long for a market
where they can chatter and laugh.

I know, I know.
Don't you think that I too know
these things? Want these things?
Long for these soft things?

Ever since our city was destroyed
by dust, by fire; ever since our empire
fell through weakened thoughts, through
quarrelling, I have longed for

markets again, for parks
where my people may walk,
for homes where they may sleep,
for lively arenas

where they may drum and dance.
Like all of you I have loved
these things, like you
I have wanted these things.

But I have not found them yet.
I have not found them yet.
Here the land is dry, the bush
brown. No sweet water flows.

Can you expect us to establish houses here?
To build a nation here? Where
will the old men feed their flocks?
Where will you make your markets?

So must we march
all the time?
Walk in this thirsty sun
all the time?

There is a land, south
of here, where it is richer.
I have heard tales told
of the mouths of great rivers

that smile; of forests
where farms may be broken;
deep lakes in these forests;
and plains where our cattle

may graze; and further on,
a place where the water
boils white at its whispering
edges.

White?
The water?

Hot
at its edges?

Is it not
Naderina, of which
the sages speak?

Perhaps
perhaps
the weak mind only seeks
towards these things

16

in dreams, in cracking sun-
light's visions; but I heard
the sound of silver run-
ning with the clink of water

as if a river were flowing
soft and always south from here.
For miles the land was brown and dry
for miles clear sky

and rock; three days we travelled, dream-
ing; heavy tongues dumb, soles and our ankles
numb, foreheads shocked with heat.
The land was empty and the

rainless arch of nothing stretching stretched
straight on. Three days we travelled, in-
steps knotted, chords of our thighs' flesh frayed
and muscles afraid of the next hot step, the next hot

slipping stone; three days we travelled
to that low sky morning when we saw the mist,
grey sticking breath,
nosing the blind earth;

heard the whisper, knew
the ground now soft and softer,
growing grassed and greener,
till we reached the White River ..

# CONFESSIONS OF
# A BORN SPECTATOR

*Ogden Nash*

One infant grows up and becomes a jockey,
Another plays basketball or hockey,
This one the prize ring hastes to enter,
That one becomes a tackle or center.
I'm just as glad as can be
That I'm not them, that they're not me.

With all my heart do I admire
Athletes who sweat for fun or hire,
Who take the field in gaudy pomp
And maim each other as they romp;
My limp and bashful spirit feeds
On other people's heroic deeds.

Now A runs ninety yards to score;
B knocks the champion to the floor;
C, risking vertebrae and spine,
Lashes his steed across the line.
You'd think my ego it would please
To swap positions with one of these.

Well, ego might be pleased enough,
But zealous athletes play so rough;
They do not ever, in their dealings
Consider one another's feelings.
I'm glad that when my struggle begins
Twixt prudence and ego, prudence wins.

When swollen eye meets gnarled fist,
When snaps the knee, and cracks the wrist,
When calm officialdom demands,
Is there a doctor in the stands?
My soul in true thanksgiving speaks
For this most modest of physiques.

Athletes, I'll drink to you or eat with you,
Or anything except compete with you;
Buy tickets worth their weight in radium
To watch you gambol in a stadium,
And reassure myself anew
That you're not me and I'm not you.


## THINGS MEN HAVE MADE

*D. H. Lawrence*

Things men have made with wakened hands, and put soft
    life into
are awake through years with transferred touch, and go on
    glowing
for long years.
And for this reason, some old things are lovely
warm still with the life of forgotten men who made them.


## THE MAN FROM
## SNOWY RIVER

*A. B. Paterson*

There was movement at the station, for the word had
    passed around
That the colt from old Regret had got away,
And had joined the wild bush horses – he was worth a
    thousand pound,
So all the cracks had gathered to the fray.
All the tried and noted riders from the stations near and
    far

Had mustered at the homestead overnight,
For the bushmen love hard riding where the wild bush
    horses are,
And the stock-horse snuffs the battle with delight.

There was Harrison, who made his pile when Pardon won
    the cup,
The old man with his hair as white as snow;
But few could ride beside him when his blood was fairly
    up –
He would go wherever horse and man could go.
And Clancy of the Overflow came down to lend a hand,
No better horseman ever held the reins;
For never horse could throw him while the saddle-girths
    would stand –
He learnt to ride while droving on the plains.

And one was there, a stripling on a small and weedy beast;
He was something like a racehorse undersized,
With a touch of Timor pony – three parts thoroughbred at
    least –
And such as are by mountain horsemen prized.
He was hard and tough and wiry – just the sort that won't
    say die –
There was courage in his quick impatient tread;
And he bore the badge of gameness in his bright and fiery
    eye,
And the proud and lofty carriage of his head.

But still so slight and weedy, one would doubt his power to
    stay,
And the old man said, 'That horse will never do
For a long and tiring gallop – lad, you'd better stop away,
Those hills are far too rough for such as you'.
So he waited, sad and wistful – only Clancy stood his
    friend –
'I think we ought to let him come,' he said;
'I warrant he'll be with us when he's wanted at the end,
For both his horse and he are mountain bred.

'He hails from Snowy River, up by Kosciusko's side,
Where the hills are twice as steep and twice as rough;
Where a horse's hoofs strike firelight from the flint stones
    every stride.
The man that holds his own is good enough.
And the Snowy River riders on the mountains make their
    home,
Where the river runs those giant hills between;
I have seen full many horsemen since I first commenced to
    roam,
But nowhere yet such horsemen have I seen.'

So he went; they found the horses by the big mimosa clump,
They raced away towards the mountain's brow,
And the old man gave his orders, 'Boys, go at them from the
    jump,
No use to try for fancy riding now.
And, Clancy, you must wheel them, try and wheel them to
    the right.
Ride boldly, lad, and never fear the spills,
For never yet was rider that could keep the mob in sight,
If once they gain the shelter of those hills.'

So Clancy rode to wheel them – he was racing on the wing
Where the best and boldest riders take their place,
And he raced his stock-horse past them, and he made the
    ranges ring
With the stockwhip, as he met them face to face.
Then they halted for a moment, while he swung the dreaded
    lash,
But they saw their well-loved mountains full in view,
And they charged beneath the stockwhip with a sharp and
    sudden dash,
And off into the mountain scrub they flew.

Then fast the horsemen followed, where the gorges deep
    and black
Resounded to the thunder of their tread,
And the stockwhips woke the echoes, and they fiercely
    answered back

From cliffs and crags that beetled overhead.
And upward, ever upward, the wild horses held their way,
Where mountain ash and kurrajong grew wide;
And the old muttered fiercely, 'We may bid the mob
    good day,
No man can hold them down the other side.'

When they reached the mountain's summit, even Clancy
    took a pull –
It well might make the boldest hold their breath;
The wild hop scrub grew thickly, and the hidden ground
    was full
Of wombat holes, and any slip was death,
But the man from Snowy River let the pony have his head,
And he swung his stockwhip round and gave a cheer,
And he raced him down the mountain like a torrent down
    its bed,
While the others stood and watched in very fear.

He sent the flint-stones flying, but the pony kept his feet,
He cleared the fallen timber in his stride,
And the man from Snowy River never shifted in his seat –
It was grand to see that mountain horseman ride.
Through the stringy-barks and saplings, on the rough and
    broken ground,
Down the hillside at a racing pace he went;
And he never drew the bridle till he landed safe and sound
At the bottom of that terrible descent.

He was right among the horses as they climbed the farther
    hill,
And the watchers on the mountain, standing mute,
Saw him ply the stockwhip fiercely; he was right among
    them still,
As he raced across the clearing in pursuit.
Then they lost him for a moment, where two mountain
    gullies met
In the ranges – but a final glimpse reveals
On a dim and distant hillside the wild horses racing yet,
With the man from Snowy River at their heels.

And he ran them single-handed till their sides were white
    with foam;
He followed like a bloodhound on their track,
Till they halted, cowed and beaten; then he turned their
    heads for home,
And alone and unassisted brought them back.
But his hardy mountain pony he could scarcely raise a
    trot,
He was blood from hip to shoulder from the spur;
But his pluck was still undaunted, and his courage fiery hot,
For never yet was mountain horse a cur.

And down by Kosciusko, where the pine-clad ridges raise
Their torn and rugged battlements on high,
Where the air is clear as crystal, and the white stars fairly
    blaze
At midnight in the cold and frosty sky,
And where around the Overflow the reed-beds sweep and
    sway
To the breezes, and the rolling plains are wide,
The Man from Snowy River is a household word today,
And the stockmen tell the story of his ride.


## MARTHA OF BETHANY

*Clive Sansom*


It's all very well
Sitting in the shade of the courtyard
Talking about your souls.
Someone's got to see to the cooking,
Standing at the oven all morning
With you two taking your ease.

It's all very well
Saying he'd be content
With bread and honey.
Perhaps he would – but I wouldn't,
Coming to our house like this,
Not giving him of our best.
Yes, it's all very well
Him trying to excuse you,
Saying your recipe's best,
Saying that I worry too much,
That I'm always anxious.
Someone's got to worry –
And double if the others don't care.
For it's all very well
Talking of faith and belief,
But what would you do
If everyone sat in the cool
Not getting their meals?
And he can't go wandering and preaching
On an empty stomach –
He'd die in the first fortnight.
Then where would you be
With all your discussions and questions
And no one to answer them? It's all very well.

## ALADDIN THROWS AWAY
## HIS LAMP

*Elias Lieberman*

A zooming overhead ... and steel-framed birds
Swoop by, intent on missions far away;
Within my room a cabinet yields words,
Sings, plays, and entertains me night or day.

To signal bells a sentiment arrives
From distant friends, I pluck a wire and talk;
A motor energizes wheels, contrives
A magic car for those who will not walk.
I turn a faucet ... cooling waters spout
And gladden throats that may be parched for thirst;
I press a button ... brilliant light pours out
Through globes of glass ... the darkness flees, accursed.
I need no lamp in which a jinn may dwell;
My commonplace outdoes his miracle.


## BIRCHES

*Robert Frost*


When I see birches bend to left and right
Across the lines of straighter darker trees,
I like to think some boy's been swinging them.
But swinging doesn't bend them down to stay.
Ice-storms do that. Often you must have seen them
Loaded with ice a sunny winter morning
After a rain. They click upon themselves
As the breeze rises, and turn many-coloured
As the stir cracks and crazes their enamel.
Soon the sun's warmth makes them shed crystal shells
Shattering and avalanching on the snowcrust –
Such heaps of broken glass to sweep away
You'd think the inner dome of heaven had fallen.
They are dragged to the withered bracken by the load,
And they seem not to break; though once they are bowed
So low for long, they never right themselves:
You may see their trunks arching in the woods
Years afterwards, trailing their leaves on the ground
Like girls on hands and knees that throw their hair
Before them over their heads to dry in the sun.

But I was going to say when Truth broke in
With all her matter-of-fact about the ice-storm
(Now am I free to be poetical?)
I should prefer to have some boy bend them
As he went out and in to fetch the cows –
Some boy too far from town to learn baseball,
Whose only play was what he found himself,
Summer or winter, and could play alone.
One by one he subdued his father's trees
By riding them down over and over again
Until he took the stiffness out of them,
And not one but hung limp, not one was left
For him to conquer. He learned all there was
To learn about not launching out too soon
And so not carrying the tree away
Clear to the ground. He always kept his poise
To the top branches, climbing carefully
With the same pains you use to fill a cup
Up to the brim, and even above the brim.
Then he flung outward feet first, with a swish,
Kicking his way down through the air to the ground.

So was I once myself a swinger of birches;
And so I dream of going back to be.
It's when I'm weary of considerations,
And life is too much like a pathless wood
Where your face burns and tickles with the cobwebs
Broken across it, and one eye is weeping
From a twig's having lashed it open,
I'd like to get away from earth a while
And then come back to begin over.
May no fate wilfully misunderstand me
And half grant what I wish and snatch me away
Not to return. Earth's the right place for love:
I don't know where it's likely to go better.
I'd like to go by climbing a high birch tree,
And climb black branches up a snow-white trunk
'Toward' heaven, till the tree could bear no more,

But dipped its top and set me down again.
That would be good both going and coming back.
One could do worse than be a swinger of birches.


# FIVE WAYS TO KILL A MAN

*Edwin Brock*


There are many cumbersome ways to kill a man.
You can make him carry a plank of wood
to the top of a hill and nail him to it. To do this
properly you require a crowd of people
wearing sandals, a cock that crows, a cloak
to dissect, a sponge, some vinegar and one
man to hammer the nails home.

Or you can take a length of steel,
shaped and chased in a traditional way,
and attempt to pierce the metal cage he wears.
But for this you need white horses,
English trees, men with bows and arrows,
at least two flags, a prince, and a
castle to hold your banquet in.

Dispensing with nobility, you may, if the wind
allows, blow gas at him. But then you need
a mile of mud sliced through with ditches,
not to mention black boots, bomb craters,
more mud, a plague of rats, a dozen songs
and some round hats made of steel.

In an age of aeroplanes, you may fly
miles above your victim and dispose of him by
pressing one small switch. All you then
require is an ocean to separate you, two
systems of government, a nation's scientists,

several factories, a psychopath and
land that no-one needs for several years.

These are, as I began, cumbersome ways
to kill a man. Simpler, direct, and much more neat
is to see that he is living somewhere in the middle
of the twentieth century, and leave him there.


## PARACHUTE

*Lenrie Peters*


Parachute men say
The first jump
Takes the breath away
Feet in the air disturbs
Till you get used to it

Solid ground
Is now where you left it
As you plunge down
Perhaps head first
As you listen to
Your arteries talking
You learn to sustain hope

Suddenly you are only
Holding an open umbrella
In a windy place
As the warm earth
Reaches out to you
Reassures you
The vibrating interim is over

You try to land
Where green grass yields
And carry your pack
Across the fields

The violent arrival
Puts out the joint
Earth has nowhere to go
You are at the starting point
Jumping across worlds
In condensed time
After the awkward fall
We are always at the starting point.

# *People and home*

## LISTENING TO THE LAND

*Martin Carter*

That night when I left you on the bridge
I bent down
Kneeling on my knee
and pressed my ear to listen to the land.

I bent down
listening to the land
but all I heard was tongueless whispering.

On my right hand was the sea behind the wall
the sea that has no business in the forest
and I bent down
listening to the land
but all I heard was tongueless whispering.

the old brick chimney barring out the city
the lantern posts like bottles full of fire
and I bent down
listening to the land
and all I heard was tongueless whispering
as if some buried slave wanted to speak again.

## THE EMIGRANTS – 2
Columbus

*Edward Brathwaite*


Columbus from his after-
deck watched stars, absorbed in water,
melt in liquid amber drifting

through my summer air.
Now with morning, shadows lifting,
beaches stretched before him cold and clear.

Birds circled flapping flag and mizzen
mast: birds harshly hawking, without fear.
Discovery he sailed for was so near.

Columbus from his after-
deck watched heights he hoped for,
rocks he dreamed, rise solid from my simple water.

Parrots screamed. Soon he would touch
our land, his charted mind's desire.
The blue sky blessed the morning with its fire.

But did his vision
fashion, as he watched the shore,
the slaughter that his soldiers

furthered here? Pike
point and musket butt,
hot splintered courage, bones

cracked with bullet shot,
tipped black boot in my belly, the
whip's uncurled desire?

Columbus from his after-
deck saw bearded fig trees, yellow pouis
blazed like pollen and thin

waterfalls suspended in the green
as his eyes climbed towards the highest ridges
where our farms were hidden.

Now he was sure
he heard soft voices mocking in the leaves.
What did this journey mean, this
new world mean: dis-
covery? Or a return to terrors
he had sailed from, known before?

I watched him pause.

Then he was splashing silence.
Crabs snapped their claws
and scattered as he walked towards our shore.


## ROOTS

*Harold M. Telemaque*


Who danced Saturday mornings
Between immortelle roots,
And played about his palate
The mellowness of cocoa beans.
Who felt the hint of the cool river,
In his blood,
The hint of the cool river
Chill and sweet.

Who followed curved shores
Between two seasons.
Who took stones in his hands
Stones white as milk.
Examining the island in his hands;
And shells,
Shells as pink as frog's eyes
From the sea.

Who saw the young corn sprout
With April rain.
Who measured the young meaning
By looking at the moon.
And walked roads a footpath's width,
And calling,
Cooed with mountain doves
Come morning time.

Who breathed mango odour
From his polished cheek.
Who followed the cus-cus weeders
In their rich performance.
Who heard the bamboo flute wailing
Fluting, wailing,
And watched the poui golden
Listening.

Who with the climbing sinews
Climbed the palm
To where the wind plays most,
And saw a chasmed pilgrimage
Making agreement for his clean return.
Whose heaviness
Was heaviness of dreams,
From drowsy gifts.

# THE SONG OF
# THE BANANA MAN

*Evan Jones*


Touris', white man, wipin' his face,
Met me in Golden Grove market place.
He looked at m' ol' clothes brown wid stain,
An' soaked right through wid de Portlan' rain,
He cas' his eye, turn' up his nose,
He says, 'You're a beggar man, I suppose?'
He says, 'Boy, get some occupation,
Be of some value to your nation.'

I said 'By God an' dis big right han'
You mus' recognize a banana man.

'Up in de hills, where de streams are cool,
An' mullet an' janga swim in de pool,
I have ten acres of mountain side,
An' a dainty-foot donkey dat I ride,
Four Gros Michel, an' four Lacatan,
Some coconut trees, and some hills of yam,
An' I pasture on dat very same lan'
Five she-goats an' a big black ram,

'Dat, by God an' dis big right han'
Is de property of a banana man.

'I leave m' yard early-mornin' time
An' set m' foot to de mountain climb,
I ben' m' back to de hot-sun toil,
An' m' cutlass rings on de stony soil,
Ploughin' an' weedin', diggin' an' plantin'
Till Massa Sun drop back o' Jim Crow mountain,
Den home again in cool evenin' time,
Perhaps whistling dis likkle rhyme,'

34

(Sung) 'Praise God an' m' big right han'
I will live an' die a banana man.

'Banana day is my special day,
I cut my stems an' I'm on m' way,
Load up de donkey, leave de lan'
Head down de hill to banana stan',
When de truck comes roun' I take a ride
All de way down to de harbour side –
Dat is de night, when you, touris' man,
Would change your place wid a banana man.

'Yes, by God, an' m' big right han'
I will live an' die a banana man.

'De bay is calm, an' de moon is bright
De hills look black for de sky is light,
Down at de dock is an English ship,
Restin' after her ocean trip,
While on de pier is a monstrous hustle,
Tallymen, carriers, all in a bustle,
Wid stems on deir heads in a long black snake
Some singin' songs dat banana man make,

'Like, (Sung) Praise God an' m' big right han'
I will live an' die a banana man.

'Den de payment comes, an' we have some fun,
Me, Zekiel, Breda and Duppy Son.
Down at de bar near United Wharf
We knock back a white rum, bus' a laugh,
Fill de empty bag for further toil
Wid saltfish, breadfruit, coconut oil.
Den head back home to m' yard to sleep,
A proper sleep dat is long an' deep.

'Yes, by God, an' m' big right han'
I will live an' die a banana man.

'So, when you see dese ol' clothes brown wid stain,
An' soaked right through wid de Portlan' rain,
Don't cas' your eye nor turn your nose,
Don't judge a man by his patchy clothes,
I'm a strong man, a proud man, an' I'm free,
Free as dese mountains, free as dis sea,
I know myself, an' I know my ways,
An' will sing with pride to de end o' my days,

(Sung) 'Praise God an' m' big right han'
I will live an' die a banana man.'


# YOU CAN'T GO
# HOME AGAIN

*Derek Walcott*


That second summer I returned. We arranged
To stay somewhere in the villages, and spent
Two days and one night there, but except
For the first few hours it was suddenly different,
As if either the country or myself had changed,
And all there is now is that we both spent
A bad night sleeping on our boots for pillows,
Hearing the restless surf until the dawn.
But it was not the same, it was like a book
You'd read sometime ago, walking on the brown
Sand, and where the sea breaks towards La Vierge,
A dead mind wondering at the restless billows;
And I left that morning with a long last look
At things that could not tell what they once had meant.

# THE LAKE ISLE

*Derek Walcott*

I watched the island narrowing, the fine
Writing of foam around the shores, then
The roads as small and casual as twine
Between the mountains; I looked until the plane
Turned to the final north and turned above
The open channel, and the quiet sea between
The fisherman's islets, until all that I love
Was lost in cloud. I watched the shallow green
That marked the places where there must be reef,
The silver glinting on the fuselage, each mile
Dividing us, and all fidelity strained
Till space would break it, and then after a while
I thought of nothing; nothing I knew would change.
When we arrived at Seawell, it had rained.

# JAMAICA ELEVATE

*Louise Bennett*

Dear Mark, me know you eye dem dark,
You glasses dem can't read,
But me haffe write an' tell you
How Jamaica dah-proceed.

So much tings happen so fas' an quick,
Me head still feel giddy!
Biff, Referandum! Buff, Election!
Baps, Independence drop pon we!

We tun Independent Nation
In de Commonwealth of Nations,
An we get congratulation
From de folks of high careers;
We got Consuls an Ambassadors,
An Ministers an Senators
Dah-rub shoulders an dip mout
Eena heavy world affairs.

We sen we Delegation
Over to United Nation,
An we meck O.A.S. know dat
We gwine join dem.
We tell Russia we don't like dem,
We tell Englan' we naw beg dem,
An we meck 'Merica know
We is behine dem.

For though we Army scanty
An we Navy don't form yet,
Any nation dat we side wid
Woulda never need to fret;

We defence is not defenceless
For we got we half o' brick,
We got we broken bottle
An we Cookoomacka stick.

But we willing to put down we arms
In Peace an Freedom's name,
An we call upon de nations
Of de worl to do de same.

We got we owna Stadium
We owna Bank fe save,
We owna National Anthem,
An we owna Flag a-wave.

We owna Govana-General,
A true-bawn Native Son;
Don't you remember Bada John-John?
Well, him fava him can't done.

De fus day him picture print, de
Paper drop out o' me han;
Me heart go boop, me bawl out
'Something bad happen to John!'

Meck dem draw him pikcha big so?
Him too ole fe pass exam.
Him noh buy noh sweepstake ticket?
Something bad happen to John!

Jamesy run come read de writin,
An it wasn' John at all;
It was we new an well appointed
Govana-General.

Jus like one o' we own fambily,
De very same complexion,
An de head part an de face part
De dead stamp o' Bada John.

So you see how we progressin,
Gi me love to Cousin Kate,
Spred de news to fren an fambily
How Jamaica elevate.

# JAMAICAN FISHERMAN

*Philip M. Sherlock*


Across the sand I saw a black man stride
    To fetch his fishing gear and broken things,
And silently that splendid body cried
    Its proud descent from ancient chiefs and kings.
Across the sand I saw him naked stride;
    Sang his black body in the sun's white light
The velvet coolness of dark forests wide,
    The blackness of the jungle's starless night.
He stood beside the old canoe which lay
Upon the beach; swept up within his arms
The broken nets and careless lounged away
Towards his wretched hut . . .
Nor knew how fiercely spoke his body then
Of ancient wealth and savage regal men.


# THE MAROON GIRL

*Walter Adolphe Roberts*


I see her on a lonely forest track,
Her level brows made salient by the sheen
Of flesh the hue of cinnamon. The clean
Blood of the hunted, vanished Arawak
Flows in her veins with blood of white and black.
Maternal, noble-breasted is her mien;
She is a peasant, yet she is a queen.
She is Jamaica poised against attack.
Her woods are hung with orchids; the still flame
Of red hibiscus lights her path, and starred
With orange and coffee blossoms is her yard.

40

Fabulous, pitted mountains close the frame.
She stands on ground for which her fathers died;
Figure of savage beauty, figure of pride.

•

## REVELATION

*H. A. Vaughan*

Turn sideways now and let them see
What loveliness escapes the schools,
Then turn again, and smile, and be
The perfect answer to those fools
Who always prate of Greece and Rome,
'The face that launched a thousand ships,'
And such like things, but keep tight lips
For burnished beauty nearer home.
Turn in the sun, my love, my love!
What palm-like grace! What poise! I swear
I prize these dusky limbs above my life.
What laughing eyes! What gleaming hair!

## STREET PREACHER

*Edward Baugh*

They are the daughters of music
On the pavements
Beating their drums
When the Sabbath sun goes down.

Who can say
If the goatskin drums
Pound their monotonous rhythm
On the heart of God?
Do the tambourines
Make a joyful noise in His ears?

## THERE WAS AN INDIAN

*Sir John Squire*

There was an Indian, who had known no change
    Who strayed content along a sunlit beach
Gathering shells. He heard a sudden strange
    Commingled noise; looked up; and gasped for speech.
For in the bay, where nothing was before,
    Moved on the sea, by magic, huge canoes,
With bellying cloth on poles, and not one oar,
    And fluttering coloured signs and clambering crews.

And he, in fear, this naked man alone,
    His fallen hands forgetting all their shells,
His lips gone pale, knelt low behind a stone,
    And stared, and saw, and did not understand
Columbus's doom-burdened caravels
    Slant to the shore, and all their seamen land.

# WORLD'S END

*G. K. Chettur*

Because, just then, I'd nothing else to do,
I laid my chin upon the study table,
And watched a crack where the tough wood had split;
And, presently, there tumbled out of it,
A little beetle striped in green and blue.
Quickly he ran as fast as he was able
To the far end; then stopped, as though his wit
Had failed him there; and then as quickly flew,
With show of confidence incomparable,
Along the very edge, till seeing me there,
He stopped again; then peeps uneasy stole,
Down o'er the edge, which to him was world's end,
And then at me again that seemed no friend;
Next, longingly, across the table, where
His home showed safe. He knew not for his soul
What next to do : to run back, or extend
Enquiry farther? – Then in sheer despair,
He gave it up, and scuttled to his hole.

# The lighter side
# of life

## THE FLEA

*Frank Collymore*

I think that I shall never see
A poem livelier than a Flea.

## THE BEE

*Frank Collymore*

Busy Bee
Don't bother me.
Being busy
Makes me dusy.
All the Bee does
Is boes ... boes ... boes.

## THE MOTH

*Frank Collymore*

The Moth
Eath Cloth.

44

# THE TERMITE

*Frank Collymore*

When once your home the Termite enters
Thenceforth you'll entertain carpenters.


# THE PIG

*Frank Collymore*

The Pig
Is very
Very
Big.
And sometimes even bigger;
For all that swallowing
And wallowing
And excessive hollering
Do nothing at all
However small
To improve his figure.


# RABBITS

*Frank Collymore*

That one and one make two
Is a rule for me and you;
But rabbits never go to school
And so they just ignore the rule.

45

Put one and one together : soon
They'll add up to a whole platoon.


## THE CRAB

*Frank Collymore*


Crabs abound by land and ocean
And they move perpetually with a sideways motion,
And when Crabs put on too much fat,
They just walk out of their skins and that is that.
But when I get too fat I either
Have to go on a diet or get new clothes, or neither.


## THE TURTLE

*Frank Collymore*


The Turtle by means of her shell provides the
        curio shop with every kind of curiosity,

The fruit of the local craftsman's ingenuity or
        (as some would have it) ingeniosity;

These numerous articles provide a wide and
        startling range or variosity,

Such as combs, trays, buttons of every size and
        description, watch-straps, necklaces,
        jewel cases, matchbox-cases, cuff-links,

46

brooches, cases for playing cards and
visiting cards, paper-knives, bookmarks,
all sorts of charms, napkin rings,
earrings, key-rings, just ordinary rings,
and many another quaint little monstrosity.


# THE SPARROWBIRD

*Frank Collymore*


I think it high time someone or other spoke an
          encouraging word
On behalf of that ubiquitous and irrepressible
          little creature, the Sparrowbird.
For although by many persons she is regarded as
          a pest
Who removes samples of their rugs or mats or
          carpets for the furnishing of her nest,
And who, by mild incursions into their comestibles
          at the breakfast table,
Earns for herself a somewhat opprobious label,
Yet let us not forget that these annoying little
          habits of hers exemplify
The subtle difference between picking and stealing
          (as the Catechism will testify).
Regard her as she alights among us, not quite
          sure whether she's going to be shoo'd,
Eying us in a manner that's at once pert and
          perky, though never downright rude,
And as she performs her deft bending and stretching
          exercises
On the rims of bowls and jugs and teacups, note
          how she emphasizes,
And thereby bears eloquent witness
To the necessity of personal fitness,

And, in short, reminds us that life is a gay
              adventure
Although there may be many a slip betwixt the
              beak and the trencher;
And, as we watch her dart through the air, let us
              not lose sight of
The fact that it's not only the Bumblebee that
              someone could write a musical composition
              on the flight of.


## IF I WERE YOU

*Frank Collymore*


If I were you and you were I
            Would we? I do not know.
For I'd be you and you'd be I
            And nothing left to show
That I was I and you were you
            Before we (you and I)
Were I and you, and so it is
            A waste of time to try
To think of what (if you were I
            And I were you) we'd do,
So better call the whole thing off
            And leave me me, you you.

# HOW McDOUGAL
# TOPPED THE SCORE

*Thomas E. Spencer*


A peaceful spot is Piper's Flat. The folk that live around –
They keep themselves by keeping sheep and turning up the
    ground;
But the climate is erratic, and the consequences are
The struggle with the elements is everlasting war.
We plough, and sow, and harrow – then sit down and pray
    for rain;
And then we all get flooded out and have to start again.
But the folk are now rejoicing as they ne'er rejoiced before,
For we've played Molongo cricket, and McDougal topped the
    score!

Molongo had a head on it, and challenged us to play
A single-innings match for lunch – the losing team to pay.
We were not great guns at cricket, but we couldn't well say
    no,
So we all began to practise, and we let the reaping go.
We scoured the Flat for ten miles round to muster up our
    men,
But when the list was totalled we could only number ten.
Then up spoke big Tim Brady : he was always slow to speak,
And he said – 'What price McDougal, who lives down at
    Cooper's Creek?'

So we sent for old McDougal, and he stated in reply
That he'd never played at cricket, but he'd half a mind to
    try.
He couldn't come to practise – he was getting in his hay,
But he guessed he'd show the beggars from Molongo how to
    play.
Now, McDougal was a Scotchman, and a canny one at that,
So he started in to practise with a paling for a bat.

He got Mrs Mac to bowl to him, but she couldn't run at all,
So he trained his sheep-dog, Pincher, how to scout and fetch
    the ball.


Now, Pincher was no puppy; he was old, and worn, and
    grey;
But he understood McDougal, and – accustomed to obey –
When McDougal cried out 'Fetch it!' he would fetch it in a
    trice,
But, until the word was 'Drop it!' he would grip it like a
    vice.
And each succeeding night they played until the light grew
    dim :
Sometimes McDougal struck the ball – sometimes the ball
    struck him.
Each time he struck, the ball would plough a furrow in the
    ground;
And when he missed, the impetus would turn him three
    times round.


The fatal day at length arrived – the day that was to see
Molongo bite the dust, or Piper's Flat knocked up a tree!
Molongo's captain won the toss, and sent his men to bat,
And they gave some leather-hunting to the men of Piper's
    Flat.
When the ball sped where McDougal stood, firm planted in
    his track,
He shut his eyes, and turned him round, and stopped it –
    with his back!
The highest score was twenty-two, the total sixty-six,
When Brady sent a yorker down that scattered Johnson's
    sticks.


Then Piper's Flat went in to bat, for glory and renown,
But, like the grass before the scythe, our wickets tumbled
    down.
'Nine wickets down for seventeen, with fifty more to win!'
Our captain heaved a heavy sigh, and sent McDougal in.

'Ten pounds to one you'll lose it!' cried a barracker from
    town;
But McDougal said, 'I'll tak' it mon!' and planked the
    money down.
Then he girded up his moleskins in a self-reliant style,
Threw off his hat and boots and faced the bowler with a
    smile.


He held the bat the wrong side out, and Johnson with a grin
Stepped lightly to the bowling crease, and sent a 'wobbler'
    in;
McDougal spooned it softly back, and Johnson waited there,
But McDougal, crying 'Fetch it!' started running like a hare.
Molongo shouted 'Victory! He's out as sure as eggs,'
When Pincher started through the crowd, and ran through
    Johnson's legs.
He seized the ball like lightning; then he ran behind a log,
And McDougal kept on running, while Molongo chased the
    dog!


They chased him up, they chased him down, they chased
    him round and then
He darted through the slip-rail as the scorer shouted 'Ten!'
McDougal puffed; Molongo swore; excitement was intense;
As the scorer marked down twenty, Pincher cleared a
    barbed-wire fence;
'Let us head him!' shrieked Molongo. 'Brain the mongrel
    with a bat!'
'Run it out! Good old McDougal!' yelled the men of Piper's
    Flat.
And McDougal kept on jogging, and then Pincher doubled
    back,
And the scorer counted 'Forty' as they raced across the
    track.


McDougal's legs were going fast, Molongo's breath was
    gone –
But still Molongo chased the dog – McDougal struggled on.

When the scorer shouted 'Fifty' then they knew the chase
  could cease,
And McDougal gasped out 'Drop it!' as he dropped within
  his crease.
Then Pincher dropped the ball, and as instinctively he knew
Discretion was the wiser plan, he disappeared from view;

And as Molongo's beaten men exhausted lay around
We raised McDougal shoulder-high, and bore him from the
  ground.

We bore him to McGinniss's, where lunch was ready laid,
And filled him up with whisky-punch, for which Molongo
  paid.
We drank his health in bumpers and we cheered him three
  times three,
And when Molongo got its breath Molongo joined the spree
And the critics say they never saw a cricket match like that,
When McDougal broke the record in the game at Piper's
  Flat;
And the folk are jubilating as they never did before;
For we played Molongo cricket – and McDougal topped the
  score!


# AT THE THEATRE
(To the lady behind me)

*A. P. Herbert*


Dear Madam, you have seen this play;
I never saw it till today.
You know the details of the plot,
But, let me tell you, I do not.
The author seeks to keep from me
The murderer's identity,

And you are not a friend of his
If you keep shouting who it is.
The actors in their funny way
Have several funny things to say,
But they do not amuse me more
If you have said them just before.
The merit of the drama lies,
I understand, in some surprise;
But the surprise must now be small
Since you have just foretold it all.
The lady you have brought with you
Is, I infer, a half-wit, too,
But I can understand the piece
Without assistance from your niece.
In short, foul woman, it would suit
Me just as well if you were mute;
In fact, to make my meaning plain,
I trust you will not speak again.
And – may I add one human touch? –
Don't breathe upon my neck so much.

# Nature, the giver,
## the teacher

---

## LITANY

*George Campbell*

I hold the splendid daylight in my hands
Inwardly grateful for a lovely day.
Thank you life.
Daylight like a fine fan spread from my hands
Daylight like scarlet poinsettia
Daylight like yellow cassia flowers
Daylight like clean water
Daylight like green cacti
Daylight like sea sparkling with white horses
Daylight like tropic hills
Daylight like a sacrament in my hands.

Amen.

## DAWN IS A FISHERMAN

*Raymond Barrow*

Dawn is a fisherman, his harpoon of light
Poised for a throw – so swiftly morning comes:
The darkness squats upon the sleeping land
Like a flung cast-net, and the black shapes of boats
Lie hunched like nesting turtles
On the flat calm of the sea.

Among the trees the houses peep at the stars
Blinking farewell, and half-awakened birds
Hurtle across the vista, some in the distance
Giving their voice self-criticised auditions.

Warning comes from the cocks, their necks distended
Like city trumpeters: and suddenly
Between the straggling fences of grey cloud
The sun, a barefoot boy, strides briskly up
The curved beach of the sky, flinging his greetings
Warmly in all directions, laughingly saying
Up, up, the day is here! Another day is here!


## NO EQUAL MESSAGE

*A. L. Hendricks*

On the untidy beach, ragged
with sea cast-offs, kelp,
drift-wood, crab-carcases, walking
I found a plain stone, dark
and smooth, polished by sand
on bleak rocks in the surf's
harsh factory; a black stone
washed cold, as only a stone is
cold, curved to an oval round,
hard and beautiful.
                              Your jewel
gleaming in the light of three candles,
upon your slim wrist, fair lady,
brings me no message equal
to sea-stories my dark stone will tell.

## NATURE

*H. D. Carberry*


We have neither Summer nor Winter
Neither Autumn nor Spring.

We have instead the days
When gold sun shines on the lush green canefields –
Magnificently.

The days when the rain beats like bullets on the roofs
And there is no sound but the swish of water in the gullies
And trees struggling in the high Jamaica winds.

Also there are the days when the leaves fade from off
    guango trees
And the reaped canefields lie bare and fallow in the sun.
But best of all there are the days when the mango and the
    logwood blossom.
When the bushes are full of the sound of bees and the scent
    of honey,
When the tall grass sways and shivers to the slightest breath
    of air,
When the buttercups have paved the earth with yellow
    stars
And beauty comes suddenly and the rains have gone.

# AUTUMN IN ENGLAND

*A. J. Seymour*


There
Daylight comes in with a flower of fountains
And sunlight stands in white unbroken columns
On the sea.
          Exiled I dream.

Down South
The masculine sun builds his strong architecture
Of heat and light, though, shouldering up, the trees
Fashion cool caves of shadow with their swaying walls
At the wind's mercy.
          But the light is deep,
And there are whirling lyrics in one's heart.

But here,
Oh, here the leaves in elegies
Drift to the iron ground, and winter's birth
Is heavy within the yellow.
          There are no winds
To shake warm curtains, and the cold
Stands round the stone and then invades the heart.

At home now
Daylight burnishes the sea
And the sun drenches the city with his warmth.

To be at home ...

# THE PAWPAW

*Edward Brathwaite*

Four little boys, tattered,
Fingers and faces splattered
With mud, had climbed
In the rain and caught
A pawpaw which they brought,
Like a bomb, to my house. I saw
Them coming : a serious, mumbling,
Tumbling bunch who stopped
At the steps in a hunch.
Releasing the fruit from the leaf
It was wrapped in, I watched them
Carefully wash the pawpaw
Like a nugget of gold. This done,
With rainwater, till it shone,
They climbed into the house
To present the present to me.
A mocking sign of the doom of all flesh?
Or the purest gold in the kingdom?


# ORDINARY EVENINGS

*A. L. Hendricks*

On this quite ordinary evening, as the habitual
        sun is reddening in the west
and small birds chatter on the high branches,
customary shadows of familiar trees
stretch upon the earth for the long night's rest.

Now the diurnal town is closing, its anxious
        stir and usual trade
drift to a crawl; only a few contentious shops
offer their thresholds; eventually all
        commerce stops:
the machine stands idle, the counter empty;
        abandoned lies the blade.

Here the warm sound of women speaking at their meal
moves gently in the air with a full calm music:
It is the time of the muted note, of the slow thick
silences of nightfall, of the stopped engine
        and the braked still wheel.

It is the time of the soundless stars, of the
        quiet watch they mount and keep
over the wide unmeasured sky;
it is the time of comprehension when patient men
        glimpse high
unplanned ambitions; and children sprawl in sweet
        untroubled sleep.


# NIGHT

*A. N. Forde*


Night ...... and the trees
Stand thankfully free
Of the day's bright boredom.

Grateful the pause
From the cruel interrogation
Of the shrill sun.

And here by the water's friendship
Pictures cross my eye-screen : the pier
Striding in dark manly courage
Out to sea; the fisher's boat
On the palm of a wave trembling;
The water lazy-lapping.

Movement gracefully sleeps
On the day's loud rhetoric.

Antithesis prevails : the firefly
A moving full-stop in the dark;

Sound an echo to sense;

And night featuring
Its grim dramatic irony :

That silence should seem
More eloquent than syllables.

That a body clothed in sin
Should be sprinkled with the dust of a star.

## MIRACLES

*Walt Whitman*

Why, who makes much of a miracle?
As to me I know of nothing else but miracles,
Whether I walk the streets of Manhattan,
Or dart my sight over the roofs of houses toward the sky,
Or wade with naked feet along the beach just in the edge of
    the water,

Or stand under trees in the woods,
Or watch honey-bees busy around the hive of a summer
   forenoon,
Or animals feeding in the fields,
Or birds, or the wonderfulness of insects in the air,
Or the wonderfulness of the sundown, or of the stars shining
   so quiet and bright,
Or the exquisite delicate thin curve of the new moon in
   spring;
These with the rest, one and all, are to me miracles,
The whole referring, yet each distinct and in its place.

To me every hour of the light and dark is a miracle,
Every cubic inch of space is a miracle,
Every square yard of the surface of the earth is spread with
   the same,
Every foot of the interior swarms with the same.

To me the sea is a continual miracle,
The fishes that swim – the rocks – the motion of the waves
   – the ships with men in them,
What stranger miracles are there?


## FLYING CROOKED

*Robert Graves*


The butterfly, a cabbage-white,
(His honest idiocy of flight)
Will never now, it is too late,
Master the art of flying straight,
Yet has – who knows so well as I? –
A just sense of how not to fly:

He lurches here and here by guess
And God and hope and hopelessness.
Even the aerobatic swift
Has not his flying-crooked gift.


LOOK, STRANGER ...

*W. H. Auden*


Look, stranger, on this island now
The leaping light for your delight discovers,
Stand stable here
And silent be,
That through the channels of the ear
May wander like a river
The swaying sound of the sea.

Here at the small field's ending pause
When the chalk wall falls to the foam and its tall ledges
Oppose the pluck
And knock of the tide,
And the shingle scrambles after the sucking surf,
And the gull lodges
A moment on its sheer side.

Far off like floating seeds the ships
Diverge on urgent voluntary errands,
And the full view
Indeed may enter
And move in memory as now these clouds do,
That pass the harbour mirror
And all the summer through the water saunter.

# THE MOON

*Soussou*

The moon lights the earth
it lights the earth but still
the night must remain the night.
The night cannot be like the day.
The moon cannot dry our washing.
Just like a woman cannot be a man
just like black can never be white.


# PRAYER FOR THE GOD THOT

*Egyptian*

The tall palm tree sixty feet high
heavy with fruit:
the fruit contains kernels,
the kernels water.
You who bring water to the remotest place

come and save me because I am humble.
O Thot, you are a sweet well
for him who starves in the desert.
A well that remains closed to the talkative

but opens up to the silent.
When the silent man approaches the well reveals itself;
when the noisy man comes you remain hidden.

# SONG FOR THE SUN
## THAT DISAPPEARED
## BEHIND THE RAINCLOUDS

*Hottentot*

The fire darkens, the wood turns black.
The flame extinguishes, misfortune upon us.
God sets out in search of the sun.
The rainbow sparkles in his hand,
the bow of the divine hunter.
He has heard the lamentations of his children.

He walks along the milky way, he collects the stars.
With quick arms he piles them into a basket
piles them up with quick arms
like a woman who collects lizards
and piles them into her pot, piles them up
until the pot overflows with lizards
until the basket overflows with light.

# Coming up against life

## POEM

*Harold M. Telemaque*

To those
Who lifted into shape
The huge stones of the pyramid;
Who formed the Sphinx in the desert,
And bid it
Look down upon the centuries like yesterday;
Who walked lithely
On the banks of the Congo,
And heard the deep rolling moan
Of the Niger;
And morning and evening
Hit the brave trail of the forest
With the lion and the elephant;
To those
Who, when it came that they should leave
Their urns of History behind,
Left only with a sad song in their hearts;
And burst forth into soulful singing
As bloody pains of toil
Strained like a hawser at their hearts ...
To those, hail ...

# LOOKING AT YOUR HANDS

*Martin Carter*

No!
I will not still my voice!
I have
too much to claim –
if you see me
looking at books
or coming to your house
or walking in the sun
know that I look for fire!

I have learnt
from books dear friend
of men dreaming and living
and hungering in a room without a light
who could not die since death was far too poor
who did not sleep to dream, but dreamed to change the
world

and so
if you see me
looking at your hands
listening when you speak
marching in your ranks
you must know
I do not sleep to dream, but dream to change the world.

# EPITAPH

*Dennis Scott*

They hanged him on a clement morning, swung
between the falling sunlight and the women's
breathing, like a black apostrophe to pain.
All morning while the children hushed
their hop-scotch joy and the cane kept growing
he hung there, sweet and low.

               At least that's how
they tell it. It was long ago
and what can we recall of a dead slave or two
except that when we punctuate our island tale
they swing like sighs across the brutal
sentences, and anger pauses
till they pass away.


# IF WE MUST DIE

*Claude McKay*

If we must die, let it not be like hogs
Hunted and penned in an inglorious spot,
While round us bark the mad and hungry dogs,
Making their mock of our accursed lot.
If we must die, O let us nobly die,
So that our precious blood may not be shed
In vain; then even the monsters we defy
Shall be constrained to honour us though dead.
As kinsmen we must meet the common foe.
Though far outnumbered let us show us brave,
And for their thousand blows deal one death blow.

What though before us lies the open grave?
Like men we'll face the murderous, cowardly pack,
Pressed to the wall, dying, but fighting back.




## ROMAN HOLIDAY

*Frank Collymore*


O, IT was a lovely funeral!
One hundred and thirty-two cars,
And three of them packed high with flowers
And the streets thronged with people –
It reminded me of the Coronation –
And then such a beautiful service:
Organ and full choir of course,
And hardly a dry eye in the chapel,
And there were so many people present that they
    all couldn't get in and ever so many of
    them had to stand outside and during the
    service there was such a hard shower,
And most of the gentlemen in morning coats and
    top hats too.
And a well-dressed respectable-looking woman
    turned to me
And asked me –
Poor creature, she could scarcely articulate
    the words –
If it was true he'd really died from what we heard,
And I told her it was only too true, poor man.
And it wasn't until afterwards that I discovered
It really wasn't *his* funeral at all.
Because there was another one that evening and they
    had both got mixed up in all the confusion;
And I do think they ought to see to it that better
    arrangements should be made –

I mean, it can put one out so;
And when I did manage to get outside and reach the
    grave
It was all over.
But it really was a lovely funeral,
And I don't know when I've cried so much.
And that reminds me, my dear:
Have you heard that his youngest daughter
Has run away
With the chauffeur?


# THE LESSON

*Edward Lucie-Smith*


'Your father's gone,' my bald headmaster said.
His shiny dome and brown tobacco jar
Splintered at once in tears. It wasn't grief.
I cried for knowledge which was bitterer
Than any grief. For there and then I knew
That grief has uses – that a father dead
Could bind the bully's fist a week or two;
And then I cried for shame, then for relief.

I was a month past ten when I learnt this:
I still remember how the noise was stilled
In school-assembly when my grief came in.
Some goldfish in a bowl quietly sculled
Around their shining prison on its shelf.
They were indifferent. All the other eyes
Were turned towards me. Somewhere in myself
Pride, like a goldfish, flashed a sudden fin.

# HURRICANE PASSAGE

*Owen Campbell*

But dawn came with a rush and lightning blazed
Far fiercer than sunflash about and above.
Music was wilder than ever, – louder.
Sky letting her tresses fly, gazed,
Glared madly at us.

Foam swirled in a ballet of waves and shouted,
And the spray hurled aloft, pirouetted.
Foam spun on before us and swirled with the wind.
We were frighted,
And lowered mainsail and jib.

                    The wind.
Horn-blasting, the wind spun away, sped in spirals,
Armed with the spray and the rain;
Struck wildly at cloud torn to tatters and tassel,
Swung again and again;

Spun a tassel-shaped cloud to the sea,
Tore a rent in the smoke
And sped through the flue that was there.
It blundered and broke.

                    The sea.
The sea gnashed its teeth at the wind,
Gaped, clacked its jaws like gunfire.
Brazen-bellied, it bellowed,
Reared higher.

The sea whirled and growled in its temper.
The sea was a hunger;
Rushed to wrestle our vessel,
Mouth agape to its iron maw.

                    The ship.
Bounded or plunged, hounded,
We yawed, but still pounded to southward.
Sea engulfed us.
And belched us again in its rage.
The day was an age.




## AT A FISHING SETTLEMENT

*Alistair Campbell*


October, and a rain-blurred face,
And all the anguish of that bitter place.
It was a bare sea-battered town
With its one street leading down
On to a shingly beach. Sea winds
Had long picked the dark hills clean
Of everything but tussock and stones
And pines that dropped small brittle cones

On to a soured soil. And old houses flanking
The street hung poised like driftwood planking
Blown together and could not outlast
The next window-shuddering blast
From the storm-whitened sea.
It was bitterly cold; I could see
Where muffled against gusty spray
She walked the clinking shingle; a stray
Dog whimpered, and pushed a small
Wet nose into my hand – that is all.
Yet I am haunted by that face,
That dog, and that bare bitter place.

# THIS ABOVE ALL IS PRECIOUS
# AND REMARKABLE

*John Wain*

This above all is precious and remarkable,
How we put ourselves in one another's care,
How in spite of everything we trust each other.

Fishermen at whatever point they are dipping and lifting
On the dark green swell they partly think of as home
Hear the gale warnings that fly to them like gulls.

The scientists study the weather for love of studying it,
And not specially for love of the fishermen,
And the wireless engineers do the transmission for love of
    wireless,

But how it adds up is that when the terrible white malice
Of the waves high as cliffs is let loose to seek a victim,
The fishermen are somewhere else and so not drowned.

And why should this chain of miracles be easier to believe
Than that my darling should come to me as naturally
As she trusts a restaurant not to poison her?

They are simply examples of well-known types of miracle,
The two of them,
That can happen at any time of the day or night.

# A SMALL TRAGEDY

*Sally Roberts*


They came up in the evening
And said to him, 'Fly!
All is discovered!'
And he fled.

A quiet little man,
Of no importance.
In fifty years he had acquired
Only flat feet and spectacles
And a distressing cough.

After a month or more,
(He having gone so quickly)
An inspector called
And they began to find the bodies.

A large number of them,
Stuffed into cupboards and corners.
(At work he was tidy
But files and paper-clips
Are matters of some importance.)

In the end, of course,
He was hanged,
Very neatly,
Though pleading insanity.

A quiet little man,
Who knew what to do with files and paper-clips,
But had no ideas about people
Except to destroy them.

# *Birds, animals and us*

## CARRION CROWS

*A. J. Seymour*

Yes, I have seen them perched on paling posts –
Brooding with evil eyes upon the road,
Their black wings hooded – and they left these roosts
When I have hissed at them. Away they strode
Clapping their wings in a man's stride, away
Over the fields. And I have seen them feast
On swollen carrion in the broad eye of day,
Pestered by flies, and yet they never ceased.

But I have seen them emperors of the sky,
Balancing gracefully in the wind's drive
With their broad sails just shifting, or again
Throwing huge shadows from the sun's eye
To brush so swiftly over the field's plain,
And winnowing the air like beauty come alive.

## BIRD

*Dennis Scott*

That day the bird hunted an empty, gleaming sky
and climbed and coiled and spun measures of joy,
half-sleeping in the sly wind way
above my friend and me. Oh,

74

its wings' wind-flick and fleche were free
and easy in the sun, and a whip's tip
tracing of pleasure its mute madrigal,
that I below watched it so tall
it could not fall save slow
down the slow day.

'What is it?' said my friend.
'Yonder ...'
                hill and home patterned and curved
and frozen in the white round air
'Yes, there,' he said, I see it –'
                            up
the steep sky till the eye
lidded from weight of sun on earth and wing!

'Watch this,' he said, bending for stones,
and my boy's throat grew tight with warning
to the bird that rode the feathered morning.

'Now there's a good shot, boy!' he said.
I was only ten then.
'If you see any more be sure to shout
but don't look at the sun too long,' he said,
'makes your eyes run.'

## NOTES FROM
## A CANADIAN DIARY

*Edward Baugh*

I.

On a day that was neither winter nor spring
A pair of gulls returned.
Today I am moved among words

Remembering
With what a tumult of delight
You greeted the event.
And as you screamed your gladness
I heard a harp
            That had been still
A winter of years
            Plucked once and fiercely.
The raptured chord
            Trembles to stillness.
Across the lake
            The wings dissolve.


II.

The park suddenly is beautiful
Where it crosses the street
And leans into the lake.
My back to the sun,
I watch my shadow lengthen.
Boys race
Rolling sideways down the slope.
A girl
Astride the life-size lion
Poses for her photograph.
The ancient citizens,
In their accustomed places,
Watch silently the sailboats
Turn into the breeze.
The boats, the boys, the girl, the ancients,
My shadow
Lenthening –
Above all this the gulls possess the hour,
The evening rosy-pink upon their breasts.


III.

Then, on a day of festivity,
I came upon a gull floating
Feet skyward by the shore.

76

Two small boys exercise their arms
With pebbles at him.
Above him, his brothers, as is their wont,
Make of existence an art ...
And there may have been a time
When I believed
That gulls go softly down
To some dark rock
To fold their wings and die.
Two men stroll briskly by
And drop an epitaph :
'Jesus, just like a dirty old paperbag!'


## SPARROWS AT TEA

*Frank Collymore*


This afternoon at four o'clock, in the
            breakfast-room
At the small round table seated, we two
Returning from our seabathe hungry, whom
            The waves have buffeted, without ado
Set to work. The sunlight steps
            Across the doorway; two sparrows follow.
One perches on a chair, the other hops
            Around; both waiting. The cheese is mellow
And the biscuits crisp. The gentian blue
            Teacups are emptied and filled again;
No words are spoken by us two.
            Only the expectant sparrows complain :
They flutter about the room, the whir
            Of their wings enormous in the cosy air;
Then back to the sunlit threshold, confer
            Excitedly, watching us gorging there.

## KOB ANTELOPE

*Yoruba*

A creature to pet and spoil
An animal with a smooth neck.
You live in the bush without getting lean.
You are plump like a newly-wedded wife.
You have more brass rings round your neck
than any woman.

When you run you spread fine dust
like a butterfly shaking its wings.
You are beautiful like carved wood.
Your eyes are gentle like a dove's.
Your neck seems long, long
to the covetous eyes of the hunter.

## THE CAT-EYED OWL

*Edward Brathwaite*

The cat-eyed owl, although so fierce
At night with kittens and with mice

In daylight may be mobbed
By flocks of little birds, and in
The market-place, be robbed

Of all his dignity and wisdom
By children market-women and malingering men

Who hoot at it and mocking its myopic
Eyes, shout: 'Look!
Look at it now, he hangs his head in

Shame.' This never happens to the eagle
Or the nightingale.


## THE EAGLE

*Lord Tennyson*

He clasps the crag with crooked hands;
Close to the sun in lonely lands,
Ringed with the azure world, he stands.

The wrinkled sea beneath him crawls;
He watches from his mountain walls,
And like a thunderbolt he falls.


## SOME NATURAL HISTORY

*Don Marquis*

the patagonian
penguin
is a most
peculiar
bird
he lives on
pussy
willows
and his tongue
is always furred
the porcupine
of chile

sleeps his life away
and that is how
the needles
get into the hay
the argentinian
oyster
is a very
subtle gink
for when he s
being eaten
he pretends he is
a skink
when you see
a sea gull
sitting
on a bald man s dome
she likely thinks
she s nesting
on her rocky
island home
do not tease
the inmates
when strolling
through the zoo
for they have
their finer feelings
the same
as me and you
oh deride not
the camel
if grief should
make him die
his ghost will come
to haunt you
with tears
in either eye
and the spirit of
a camel
in the midnight gloom

can be so very
cheerless
as it wanders
round the room


## SNAKE

*D. H. Lawrence*


A snake came to my water-trough
On a hot, hot day, and I in pyjamas for the heat,
To drink there.

In the deep, strange-scented shade of the great dark carob-
    tree
I came down the steps with my pitcher
And must wait, must stand and wait, for there he was at
    the trough before me.

He reached down from a fissure in the earth-wall in the
    gloom
And trailed his yellow-brown slackness soft-bellied down,
    over the edge of the stone trough
And rested his throat upon the stone bottom,

And where the water had dripped from the tap, in a small
    clearness,
He sipped with his straight mouth,
Softly drank through his straight gums, into his slack long
    body,
Silently.

Someone was before me at my water-trough,
And I, like a second comer, waiting.

He lifted his head from his drinking, as cattle do
And looked at me vaguely, as drinking cattle do,
And flickered his two-forked tongue from his lips, and
    mused a moment,
And stooped and drank a little more,
Being earth-brown, earth-golden from the burning bowels
    of the earth
On the day of Sicilian July, with Etna smoking.

The voice of my education said to me
He must be killed,
For in Sicily the black, black snakes are innocent, the gold
    are venomous.

And voices in me said, If you were a man
You would take a stick and break him now, and finish him
    off.

But must I confess how I liked him,
How glad I was he had come like a guest in quiet, to drink
    at my water-trough
And depart peaceful, pacified, and thankless,
Into the burning bowels of this earth?

Was it cowardice, that I dared not kill him?
Was it perversity, that I longed to talk to him?
Was it humility, to feel so honoured?
I felt so honoured.

And yet those voices:
*If you were not afraid, you would kill him!*
And truly I was afraid, I was most afraid,
But even so, honoured still more
That he should seek my hospitality
From out the dark door of the secret earth.

He drank enough
And lifted his head, dreamily, as one who has drunken,
And flickered his tongue like a forked night on the air, so
    black,

Seeming to lick his lips,
And looked around like a god, unseeing, into the air,
And slowly turned his head,
And slowly, very slowly, as if thrice adream,
Proceeded to draw his slow length curving round
And climb again the broken bank of my wall-face.

And as he put his head into that dreadful hole,
And as he slowly drew up, snake-easing his shoulders, and
 entered farther,
A sort of horror, a sort of protest against his withdrawing
 into that horrid black hole,
Deliberately going into the blackness, and slowly drawing
 himself after,
Overcame me now his back was turned.

I looked round, I put down my pitcher,
I picked up a clumsy log
And threw it at the water-trough with a clatter.

I think it did not hit him,
But suddenly the part of him that was left behind convulsed
 in undignified haste,
Writhed like lightning, and was gone
Into the black hole, the earth-lipped fissure in the wall-front,
At which, in the intense still noon, I stared with fascination.

And immediately I regretted it.
I thought how paltry, how vulgar, what a mean act!
I despised myself and the voices of my accursed human
 education.
And I thought of the albatross,
And I wished he would come back, my snake.

For he seemed to me again like a king,
Like a king in exile, uncrowned in the underworld,
Now due to be crowned again.

And so, I missed my chance with one of the lords
Of life.
And I have something to expiate;
A pettiness.

## THE FLATTERED
## FLYING-FISH

*E. V. Rieu*

Said the Shark to the Flying-Fish over the phone :
'Will you join me tonight? I am dining alone.
Let me order a nice little dinner for two!
And come as you are, in your shimmering blue.'

Said the Flying-Fish : 'Fancy remembering me,
And the dress that I wore at the Porpoises' tea!'
'How could I forget?' said the Shark in his guile :
'I expect you at eight!' and rang off with a smile.

She has powdered her nose; she has put on her things;
She is off with one flap of her luminous wings.
O little one, lovely, light-hearted and vain,
The Moon will not shine on your beauty again!

# SEA SCHOOL

*Barbara Howes*

This afternoon I swam with a school of fish.
Waiting in shallow water for the tide to change,
They swept at leisure through their green pleasance,
Turning at will as one, or at some private
Signal all felt;
White and delicate, each one bedizened
By an ochre spot behind his sickle of gill,
Pale translucent fish they were, divided
By the hair-thin mustache-line of backbone.

We plied our way along, taking our ease
In concert, as a school,
Feeling the flickering lozenges of light –
Chicken wire of sunlight grazing us
As we passed up and down under its stroke.
So for an hour, an age, I swam with them,
One with the rhythm of the sea, weightless,
Graceful and casual in our schoolhood,
Within our coop of light,
One with a peace that might go on forever. . . .
Till, of a sudden, quick as a falling net,
Some thought embraced them. I watched them go
Tidily over the reef, where I could not follow.

# FOR A FIVE-YEAR OLD

*Fleur Adcock*

A snail is climbing up the window-sill
Into your room, after a night of rain.
You call me in to see, and I explain
That it would be unkind to leave it there:
It might crawl to the floor; we must take care
That no one squashes it. You understand,
And carry it outside, with careful hand,
To eat a daffodil.

I see, then, that a kind of faith prevails:
Your gentleness is moulded still by words
From me, who have trapped mice and shot wild birds,
From me, who drowned your kittens, who betrayed
Your closest relatives, and who purveyed
The harshest kind of truth to many another.
But that is how things are: I am your mother,
And we are kind to snails.

# Looking back

I SHALL REMEMBER

*H. D. Carberry*


And so I leave this island –
This island that I have loved,
This people that I have loved.

But I shall remember always
The beauty of my people
And the beauty of my land.

And in strange lands
Where the fog presses down
And even the street lamps are faint and misty,
I shall remember
The beauty of our nights,
With stars so near
That one could almost stretch and touch them,
Stars – winking and flashing
Magnificently – in a sky of velvet blue.

I shall remember
Walking down long avenues of trees,
The black asphalt flecked with pale moonlight
Pouring through the acacia leaves –
And the soft laughter of girls
Leaning back, cool and inviting
Against the trunks of flaming poinciana trees.

And in the long days when the rain falls sullenly
And no sun shines
And all the earth lies in a weary stupor
I shall remember

The splendour of our sun
The brightness of our days.

And how the rain poured down
Upon a passionate thirsty earth,
Swiftly, unrelenting, with immeasurable power,
Then vanished suddenly in a peal of childlike laughter
And all the earth was green and light once more.

I shall remember
The warmth of our island seas,
The sparkling whiteness of the breaking waves
And the blue haze on our hills and mountains
With their noisy streams cascading down
Sheer cliffs, in clouds of incandescent spray
And deafening sound.

And in strange cities
Among unaccustomed people
Who move palefaced with tired staring eyes
I shall remember
The warmth and gaiety of my people
The polyglot colour and variety of their faces
The happy fusion of our myriad races
In the common love that unites and binds us to this land.

And I shall yearn for the sight
Of faces black and bronzed,
People with dark sparkling eyes
With ready tongue
And laughter loud and unashamed.

I shall remember
The faces of the women from the hills
Bringing down strange fruits
To Saturday's markets.

I shall remember
The tread of their feet on the naked earth
Their unconscious strength and poise,

As with basket bearing head thrown back,
They stride to town
Like Israel to the promised land.

Yes, I shall remember always
This my island and my people
And I shall remember always
The beauty of my people and my land.


# FLAME-HEART

*Claude McKay*


So much have I forgotten in ten years,
So much in ten brief years! I have forgot
What time the purple apples come to juice,
And what month brings the shy forget-me-not.
I have forgot the special, startling season
Of the pimento's flowering and fruiting;
What time of year the ground doves brown the fields
And fill the noonday with their curious fluting.
I have forgotten much, but still remember
The poinsettia's red, blood-red in warm December.

I still recall the honey-fever grass,
But cannot recollect the high days when
We rooted them out of the pingwing path
To stop the mad bees in the rabbit pen.
I often try to think in what sweet month
The languid painted ladies used to dapple
The yellow by-road mazing from the main,
Sweet with the golden threads of the rose-apple.
I have forgotten – strange – but quite remember
The poinsettia's red, blood-red in warm December.

What weeks, what months, what time of the mild year
We cheated school to have our fling at tops?
What days our wine-thrilled bodies pulsed with joy
Feasting upon blackberries in the copse?
Oh some I know! I have embalmed the days
Even the sacred moments when we played,
All innocent of passion, uncorrupt,
At noon and evening in the flame-heart's shade.
We were so happy, happy, I remember,
Beneath the poinsettia's red in warm December.


## THE LIME-TREE

*Edward Lucie-Smith*


The lime-tree fruited in our poultry yard;
Sometimes I dream and see it; still quite small,
I stand in nightclothes, barefoot; on the ground
My shadow stretches, shaped like a hunched bird
And cast by moonlight; then I'm tiptoe tall
To take one of the limes into my hand.

It's best the dream ends there: that now the fowls
Their draggled plumage turned to silvery mail,
Don't rouse to mock me as I slip on dung
While tugging at the fruit – I fall, it rolls
Out of my reach; the hens more coarsely rail –
I try to shout them down, can't find my tongue.

Salt on my lips I taste my silent tears;
The deep sobs rack me, choke me till I wake
To find the hand still clenched that held the cheat;
All day that hand will show four sickle scars
Upon the palm, and, as I wait day-break,
Perfume of lime clings like the sweaty sheet.

# JUNE BUG

*Edward Lucie-Smith*

Bug like a coffee-bean
Thrown on this tabletop
Beside my paper and pen,
You startle me with your rap.

You, on this hot June night
Which opens window and door,
Come like an intimate
From June of a former year.

Then I, a boy with a book
In a room where a bare bulb glared,
Slept – and struggled awake;
Round me the june bugs whirred.

And, by the inkwell, one
Trundled, a frill of wing
Glinting like cellophane:
On the very lip he clung ...

You're off? No reason to feel
That *you*, sir, stand on the brink
Of some disastrous fall
Into a pool of ink.

# THE ROAD

*Reginald M. Murray*

The moon sails o'er Long Mountain, and lights a sand-
strip lone,
Where surf swims, silver shimmering, and shoreward
breakers drone :
Along the forlorn stretches the night winds sweep and
moan :
A shadow moves, slow creeping, athwart the whiteness
thrown :
It speeds, it stops, and peers : a lance uplifts and stabs :
An Indian, silent, naked, hunting and spearing crabs.

A brigantine rides dipping, beneath the tropic moon,
With Spanish loot full laden, mantilla and doubloon,
For Morgan makes Port Royal, and bottles clink and clash,
And sailormen are cheering to see the shore-lights flash,
Carina, dark eyes glittering, bedecked with jingling rings,
Flutters to greet a gallant lad who many a moidore brings.

The self-same moon is lamping that gleaming arm to-night
Fanned by Caribbean breezes and curved for heart's delight,
But with the salt wind's sighing the sounds of laughter come
From dance-hall and from night-club, and motors throb and
hum.
For man has built a roadway, a thoroughfare, you know,
Where Indian chevied scuttling crab a mort of years ago.

# ANCESTORS

*Edward Brathwaite*

2

All that I can remember of his wife,
my father's mother, is that she sang us songs
('Great Tom Is Cast' was one), that frightened me.
And she would go chug chugging with a jar
of milk until its white pap turned to yellow
butter. And in the basket underneath the stairs
she kept the polish for grandfather's shoes.

All that I have of her is voices:
laughing me out of fear because a crappaud
jumped and splashed the dark where I was huddled
in the galvanized tin bath; telling us stories
round her fat white lamp. It was her Queen
Victoria lamp, she said; although the stamp
read Ever Ready. And in the night I listened to her singing
in a Vicks and Vapour Rub-like voice what you would call
                                                    the blues.

# CALIBAN
Limbo

*Edward Brathwaite*

And limbo stick is the silence in front of me
*limbo*

*limbo*
*limbo like me*
*limbo*
*limbo like me*

long dark night is the silence in front of me
*limbo*
*limbo like me*

stick hit sound
and the ship like it ready

stick hit sound
and the dark still steady

*limbo*
*limbo like me*

long dark deck and the water surrounding me
long dark deck and the silence is over me

*limbo*
*limbo like me*

stick is the whip
and the dark deck is slavery

stick is the whip
and the dark deck is slavery

*limbo*
*limbo like me*

drum stick knock
and the darkness is over me

knees spread wide
and the water is hiding me

*limbo*
*limbo like me*

knees spread wide
and the dark ground is under me

94

down
down
down

and the drummer is calling me

*limbo*
*limbo like me*

sun coming up
and the drummers are praising me

out of the dark
and the dumb gods are raising me

up
up
up

and the music is saving me

hot
slow
step

on the burning ground.

# NIKKI-ROSA

*Nikki Giovanni*


childhood remembrances are always a drag
if you're Black
you always remember things like living in Woodlawn
with no inside toilet
and if you become famous or something
they never talk about how happy you were to have your
  mother
all to yourself and
how good the water felt when you got your bath from
  one of those
big tubs that folk in chicago barbecue in
and somehow when you talk about home
it never gets across how much you
understood their feelings
as the whole family attended meetings about Hollydale
and even though you remember
your biographers never understand
your father's pain as he sells his stock
and another dream goes
and though you're poor it isn't poverty that
concerns you
and though they fought a lot
it isn't your father's drinking that makes any difference
but only that everybody is together and you
and your sister have happy birthdays and very good
  christmasses
and I really hope no white person ever has cause to write
  about me
because they never understand Black love is Black wealth
  and they'll
probably talk about my hard childhood and never under-
  stand that
all the while I was quite happy

# LIES

*Y. Yevtushenko*

Telling lies to the young is wrong.
Proving to them that lies are true is wrong.
Telling them that God's in his heaven
and all's well with the world is wrong.
The young know what you mean. The young are people.
Tell them difficulties can't be counted,
and let them see not only what will be
but see with clarity these present times.
Say obstacles exist they must encounter
sorrow happens, hardship happens.
The hell with it. Who never knew
the price of happiness will not be happy.
Forgive no error you recognize,
it will repeat itself, increase,
and afterwards our pupils
will not forgive in us what we forgave.


# THE BEST OF SCHOOL

*D. H. Lawrence*

The blinds are drawn because of the sun,
And the boys and the room in a colourless gloom
Of underwater float: bright ripples run
Across the walls as the blinds are blown
To let the sunlight in; and I,
As I sit on the shores of the class, alone,
Watch the boys in their summer blouses
As they write, their round heads busily bowed:

And one after another rouses
His face to look at me,
To ponder very quietly,
As seeing, he does not see.

And then he turns again, with a little, glad
Thrill of his work he turns again from me,
Having found what he wanted, having got what was to be
    had.

And very sweet it is, while the sunlight waves
In the ripening morning, to sit alone with the class
And feel the stream of awakening ripple and pass
From me to the boys, whose brightening souls it laves
For this little hour.

                    This morning, sweet it is
To feel the lads' looks light on me,
Then back in a swift, bright flutter to work;
Each one darting away with his
Discovery, like birds that steal and flee.

Touch after touch I feel on me
As their eyes glance at me for the grain
Of rigour they taste delightedly.
As tendrils reach out yearningly,
Slowly rotate till they touch the tree
That they cleave unto, and up which they climb
Up to their lives – so they to me.

I feel them cling and cleave to me
As vines going eagerly up; they twine
My life with other leaves, my time
Is hidden in theirs, their thrills are mine.

# A KIND OF HERO

*Vernon Scannell*

At school he was revered, yet lonely.
No other boy, however much
He might dream of it,
Dared to try to be his friend.
He walked, gaunt and piratical,
All bones and grin,
Towards his inescapable end.

Revered, but not by authority,
He poured ink into the new hat
Of the French master,
Painted the blackboard white,
Swore at the huge Principal,
Refused to bend
And invited him to a free fight.

In memory he is beautiful,
But only his desperate gold
Hair might have been so.
Vaguely we understood,
And were grateful that he performed
Our lawless deeds;
Punished, he allowed us to be good.

The end : he was killed at Alamein.
He wore handcuffs on the troopship
Going out, his webbing
All scrubbed as white as rice;
And we, or others like us,
Were promoted
By his last derisive sacrifice.

# INDEX OF FIRST LINES

# ACKNOWLEDGMENTS

The Publisher's thanks are due to the following for permission to use copyright material:

Meulenhoff Nederland n.v. for Bertus Aafjes' 'Prayer to the God Thot'; A. H. and A. W. Reed, N. Z. for Fleur Adcock's 'For a Five-Year-Old'; Faber & Faber Ltd for W. H. Auden's 'On this Island' from *Collected Shorter Poems 1927–1957*; Cambridge University Press for the Yoruba poem 'Kob Antelope' from Ulli Beier's *African Poetry*; Sangster's Book Stores Ltd, Kingston, Jamaica, for Louise Bennett's 'Jamaica Elevate'; Oxford University Press for verse 3 'Caliban' from *Limbo*, verse 2 from 'Ancestors' from Edward Brathwaite's *Islands*, verse 2 from 'The Emigrants' from *Rights of Passage*, 'Volta' from *Masks*, Alistair Campbell's 'At a Fishing Settlement' from *Wild Honey* and Edward Lucie-Smith's 'The Lesson', 'The Lime Tree', and 'June Bug' from *A Tropical Childhood and Other Poems*; Scorpion Press for Edwin Brock's 'Five Ways to Kill a Man' from *With Love from Judas*; Jonathan Cape for Derek Walcott's 'A Sea-Chantey' from *In a Green Night*; Robert Graves for 'Flying Crooked' and 'The Beach' from *Collected Poems 1965*; Random House Inc. and John Schaffner for 'Looking up at Leaves' © 1966; Sir Alan Herbert and Ernest Benn Ltd for 'At the Theatre' from *A Book of Ballads*; Andre Deutsch for A. L. Hendricks' 'Ordinary Evenings' and 'Road to Lacovia' from *On this Mountain*; Evan Jones for 'The Song of the Banana Man', first published by *Bim*, Bridgetown, Barbados (1952); Wm Heinemann Ltd for D. H. Lawrence's 'Things Men have Made', 'The Best of School'; and 'Snake' from *The Complete Poems of D. H. Lawrence*; Mrs Rose Lieberman for Elias Lieberman's 'Aladdin Throws away his Lamp'; Doubleday Co. Inc. for Don Maquis' 'Some Natural History'; J. M. Dent for an extract from Ogden Nash's *Confessions of a Born Spectator*; W. H. Oliver and the Caxton Press for 'The Beachcomber'; Heinemann Educational Books for Lenrie Peters' 'Parachute'; Angus & Robertson for A. B. Paterson's 'The Man from Snowy River' and Judith Wright's 'The Surfer' from *The Moving Image* (Meanjin Press); Wm Heinemann for James Reeves' 'The Sea' from *The Wandering Moon*; Methuen & Co. for E. V. Rieu's 'The Flattered Flying Fish' and Clive Sansom's 'Martha of Bethany' from *The Witnesses & Other Poems*; Vernon Scannell for 'A Kind of Hero'; Macmillan & Co. for Sir John Squire's 'The Ship' and 'There was an India' from *Collected Poems* and John Wain's 'This Above All' from *Weep before God*; Jonathan Cape and the Estate of Robert Frost for 'Birches' from *The Poetry of Robert Frost*, ed. E. C. Lathem; the Nonesuch Press for Walt Whitman's 'Miracles' from *Walt Whitman* : Complete Poetry and Selected Prose and Letters, ed. Emory Holloway and Penguin Books Ltd for Yevgeny Yevtushenko's 'Lies' from *Selected Poems of Yevtushenko*, trans. Robin Milner-Gulland and Peter Levi, S. J.

The following authors have also granted us permission to use their poems : Edward Brathwaite for 'The Cat-Eyed Owl' and 'Pawpaw'; Raymond Barrow for 'Dawn is a Fisherman'; Edward Baugh for 'Notes from a Canadian Diary' and 'Street Preacher'; Owen Campbell for lines from 'Hurricane Passage' and 'The Vessels'; George Campbell for 'Litany'; H. D. Carberry for 'Nature' and 'I Shall Remember'; Martin Carter for 'Looking at Your Hands', 'Listening to the Land', and 'Fragment of Memory'; Frank Collymore for thirteen poems; A. L. Hendricks for 'No Equal Message'; Frederick Murray for Reginald Murray's 'The Road'; Carl Cowl for Claude McKay's 'Flame-Heart' and 'If We Must Die'; C. Bernard Lewis for Adolphe Roberts' 'Maroon Girl'; Sally Roberts for 'A Small Tragedy'; Dennis Scott for 'Bird' and 'Epitaph'; A. J. Seymour for 'Buttercup', 'Carrion Crows', 'Autumn in England', and 'For Christopher Columbus'; Sir Philip Sherlock for 'Jamaican Fisherman'; H. M. Telamaque for 'Roots' and 'Poem'; H. A. Vaughan for 'Revelation'; and Derek Walcott for 'You Can't Go Home' and 'The Lake Isle'.